MIAMI HURRICANES

BY
GORDON OWENS

INSIDE COLLEGE FOOTBALL

MEDIA ENHANCED BOOKS
AV² BY WEIGL
ADDED VALUE • AUDIO VISUAL

www.av2books.com

Published by AV^2 by Weigl
350 5th Avenue, 59th Floor
New York, NY 10118
Website: www.av2books.com

Library of Congress Control Number: 2018968206

ISBN 978-1-7911-0090-2 (hardcover)
ISBN 978-1-7911-0091-9 (multi-user eBook)
ISBN 978-1-7911-0092-6 (single-user eBook)

Printed in Guangzhou, China
1 2 3 4 5 6 7 8 9 0 23 22 21 20 19

042019
102318

Project Coordinator: Jared Siemens   Designer: Terry Paulhus

Every reasonable effort has been made to trace ownership and to obtain permission to reprint copyright material. The publishers would be pleased to have any errors or omissions brought to their attention so that they may be corrected in subsequent printings.

The publisher acknowledges Alamy, Getty Images, and Wikimedia Commons as its primary image suppliers for this title.

INSIDE COLLEGE FOOTBALL

Miami Hurricanes

CONTENTS

Introduction

The University of Miami (UM) Hurricanes are a high-ranking college football team. They have won a total of four National Championships. Many Miami players go on to join the National Football League (NFL) and have long and productive careers with professional teams.

One of the Hurricanes' major **rivals** is another Florida team. The Florida State University Seminoles and the Hurricanes have been rivals since the 1950s. The Hurricanes have won 33 of their 63 games against the Seminoles. The games are often close in score, and many have become **legends** for Miami fans because of shocking endings and unbelievable plays. Miami currently has a two-game win streak against the Seminoles.

Running back Travis Homer has played in almost every game for Miami since his first season as a true freshman. Homer's 1,995 total rushing yards over three seasons are the 12th highest in Hurricanes history.

The Hurricanes live up to their name. When they enter the field at their home stadium, smoke billows from the tunnel and the sounds of a hurricane play from speakers near the entrance. Often, Hurricanes fans can be seen holding up four fingers. This tradition began because the Hurricanes often win games in the fourth quarter. Even if their team is trailing, the fans know the Hurricanes are playing to win.

In his final season with the Hurricanes, defensive back Sheldrick Redwine logged 64 total tackles, including 3.5 tackles for loss and three sacks. Redwine also had three interceptions and a fumble recovery.

MIAMI

Stadium Hard Rock Stadium

Division Atlantic Coast Conference (ACC) Coastal

Head Coach Manny Diaz

Location Miami, Florida

National Championships 4

Nicknames Hurricanes, Canes, UM

19 Bowl Victories

2 Home Stadiums

25 Head Coaches

4 Retired Numbers

History

In a 1996 game against the West Virginia University Mountaineers, Miami **blocked** a West Virginia punt and scored a touchdown with 29 seconds left. Miami won 10–7, and the game is known as the "**Miracle in Morgantown.**"

The Hurricanes began the 1983 season unranked, and played their way to a fifth-place ranking and a spot in the Orange Bowl. Miami defeated the top-ranked University of Nebraska Cornhuskers 31–30 to secure its first-ever National Championship title.

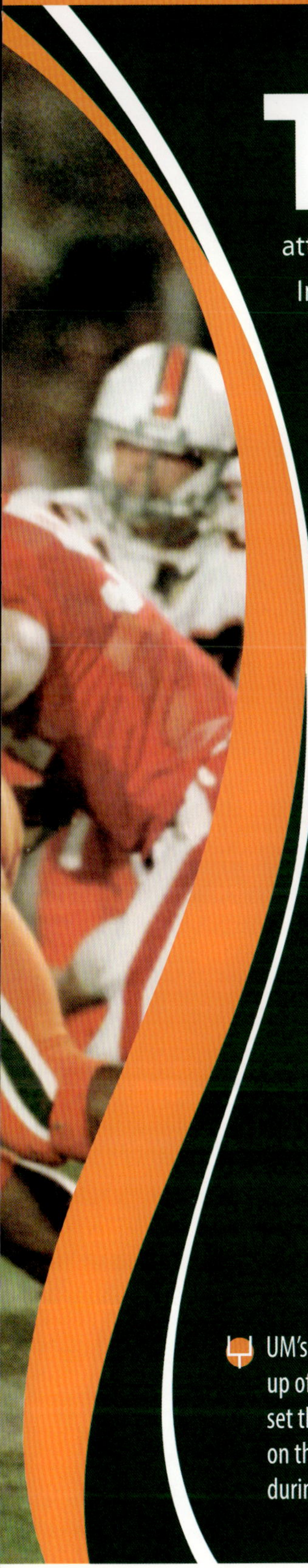

The Miami Hurricanes played their first game on October 23, 1926, barely a month after a hurricane blew through the city. The team beat Rollins College 7–0, with only 304 fans in attendance. Not all of the Hurricanes' early games were so successful. In 1930, they lost 34–0 to Temple University.

In 1937, the Hurricanes won their first Southern Intercollegiate Athletic Association Championship. At that time, the University of Miami was **segregated**. It finally became **integrated** in 1961. It took another five years for Ray Bellamy to become the first African American player on the football team. He was awarded a full scholarship to play football. Later, Bellamy became the first African American student body president at the university.

The Hurricanes won their first National Championship in 1983 under Coach Howard Schnellenberger. Four years later, in 1987, they won their second. In 1991, the Hurricanes went the whole season undefeated. In 2004, six Hurricane players were selected in the first round of the NFL **draft**. This was the most of any college in National Collegiate Athletic Association (NCAA) history. Although their first years were hard, the Hurricanes have risen to the national stage as a winning team.

UM's first football team was made up of all freshmen players. They set the stage for future success on the field with an 8–0 record during the 1926 inaugural season.

The Stadium

Although Hard Rock Stadium's seating capacity is about 65,000, there have been games where 80,000 fans have filled the stands.

In 1926, the University of Miami started building its first stadium. It was supposed to be temporary and seat 8,000 people. On the second day of construction, a hurricane known as the "Great Miami Hurricane" made landfall in South Florida. Construction on the stadium stopped. In 1937, the team moved to a new stadium. It had been built by the city, but became the home of the university football team. At the time, it was called the Roddy Burdine Municipal Stadium. In 1959, its name was changed to the Miami Orange Bowl. The Hurricanes played there for 70 years.

In 2008, the Hurricanes moved to Dolphin Stadium. Opened in 1987 as the Joe Robbie Stadium, it is also home to the NFL's Miami Dolphins. The stadium went through several name changes. Finally, in 2015, it was named the Hard Rock Stadium and is still known by that name today. In 2016, the stadium received a $550 million **renovation**. Today, it has 64,767 seats and 2,000 flat-screen monitors. Hard Rock Stadium has hosted the World Series twice and the **Super Bowl** five times, and is scheduled to host the 2020 Super Bowl, as well.

The Miami Orange Bowl was demolished in 2008. Marlins Park, home of Major League Baseball's Miami Marlins, was built in its place.

Where They Play

Welcome to Hard Rock Stadium, home of the Miami Hurricanes. The teal-green seats are crowded with fans dressed in orange. Smoke and the sounds of a hurricane fill the air. The team takes the field as the Frost Band of the Hour plays. The Hurricanes are ready to win.

ACC ATLANTIC

1 **Boston College**
Chestnut Hill, Massachusetts

2 **Clemson University**
Clemson, South Carolina

3 **Florida State University**
Tallahassee, Florida

4 **North Carolina State University**
Raleigh, North Carolina

5 **Syracuse University**
Syracuse, New York

6 **University of Louisville**
Louisville, Kentucky

7 **University of Notre Dame**
Notre Dame, Indiana

8 **Wake Forest University**
Winston-Salem, North Carolina

Arena
Hard Rock Stadium

Location
Miami, Florida

Broke Ground
July 1985

Completed
1987

Surface
Real Grass

Features
- Was home to Major League Baseball's Florida Marlins from 1993 to 2011
- Luxury boxes are "living rooms" with recliners and televisions overlooking the field
- Stadium cover shades 92 percent of the seats

ACC COASTAL

1 **Duke University**
Durham, North Carolina

2 **Georgia Institute of Technology**
Atlanta, Georgia

★3 **University of Miami**
Coral Gables, Florida

4 **University of North Carolina at Chapel Hill**
Chapel Hill, North Carolina

5 **University of Pittsburgh**
Pittsburgh, Pennsylvania

6 **University of Virginia**
Charlottesville, Virginia

7 **Virginia Polytechnic Institute and State University**
Blacksburg, Virginia

NEW HAMPSHIRE
MAINE
VERMONT
MASSACHUSETTS
RHODE ISLAND
CONNECTICUT
NEW YORK
NEW JERSEY
DELAWARE
MARYLAND
WASHINGTON, D.C.
PENNSYLVANIA
NORTH DAKOTA
SOUTH DAKOTA
MINNESOTA
WISCONSIN
MICHIGAN
IOWA
NEBRASKA
OHIO
ILLINOIS
INDIANA
WEST VIRGINIA
VIRGINIA
KENTUCKY
KANSAS
MISSOURI
NORTH CAROLINA
TENNESSEE
SOUTH CAROLINA
OKLAHOMA
ARKANSAS
MISSISSIPPI
ALABAMA
GEORGIA
TEXAS
LOUISIANA
FLORIDA
Atlantic Ocean
Gulf of Mexico
1
2
3
4
5
6
7
8
LEGEND
Home Stadium
ACC Atlantic
ACC Coastal
United States
Other Countries
Water
SCALE
0 miles
500 miles
0 kilometers
500 km
N
S
E
W

The Uniforms

The **first** helmets worn by the Hurricanes in the 1930s were **all white.**

Miami's eco-friendly uniforms were auctioned off during the 2018 season, and all of the proceeds were donated to the university's Rosenstiel School of Marine and Atmospheric Science for educational research.

The University of Miami's school colors are orange, green, and white. All of the school's uniforms use these colors. Its early uniforms included orange jerseys with green stripes on the sleeves and tan pants. Throughout the years, the Hurricanes' jerseys have varied between green, white, and orange.

The Hurricanes wear many different uniforms. The jerseys and pants can be orange, white, black, or green. Miami's helmets are typically white, although some alternate uniforms include a black helmet. Every helmet has the school **logo** on it, an orange and green "U".

One of Miami's 2018 alternate uniforms was made using 70 percent ECONYL yarn, which is made of recycled plastic from the ocean. The gloves were also made of marine plastic waste. Because the University of Miami is located so close to the beach, responsible ocean care is important to the team. The Hurricanes wear these uniforms to express their concern for the environment.

After several years of logo changes, the "split U" logo became Miami's official logo in 1973 and has changed very little since then.

Student Athletes

In 2018, student athletes at the University of Miami won the **NCAA Team Works Helper Community Service Competition Award**, recognizing their community outreach.

- Three Miami football players were named to the All-ACC Academic Team for 2018. Athletes who are named to the All-ACC Academic Team have maintained a B average or higher throughout their entire college career.

Being a college student athlete is hard work. Student athletes have to perform well on the football field and in the classroom. University of Miami student athletes are required to meet a minimum grade point average and attend all of their classes. They must also have 12 academic credits per term. Miami student athletes have access to academic advisors and tutors. The school requires freshmen student athletes to attend tutoring sessions. The University of Miami offers many other services to help players balance the student athlete life.

Many student athletes are given athletic scholarships. An athletic scholarship is a financial aid agreement between the athlete and the college or university. Athletes who do not receive an athletic scholarship can be "walk-on" members of the team. This means they are on the team, but without athletic financial aid. The University of Miami typically awards the maximum number of football scholarships allowed, which is 85.

Offensive lineman Tyree St. Louis came to Miami from the IMG Academy, a preparatory boarding school in Bradenton, Florida. IMG offers programs in eight different sports, including a football academy.

Bowl Games

The Miami Hurricanes were **ranked number-one** and were enjoying a 34-game winning streak when they lost the National Championship title to the Ohio State University Buckeyes in the **2003 Fiesta Bowl**.

Miami was unranked with an 8–4 overall record going into the 2016 Russell Athletic Bowl against number-14 West Virginia University Mountaineers. The Hurricanes defeated the Mountaineers to secure their 19th bowl victory in team history.

After the college football season ends, a rare sports tradition begins. There is no NCAA-sponsored **postseason** for the sport of football. Instead, a variety of games called bowl games are played. There are currently 40 bowl games played between college football teams. These games give teams the chance to play rivals or new teams. It is also a chance to compete for respect and wins even after they have finished with the regular season.

The Miami Hurricanes played their first bowl game in 1933, against Manhattan College. It was called the Palm Festival and was held in their hometown of Miami. The Hurricanes won 7–0. Later, this game was renamed the Orange Bowl. They have won the Orange Bowl six times since then. On December 28, 2016, the Hurricanes won the Russell Athletic Bowl, beating the West Virginia University Mountaineers 31–14. UM was trailing early in the game but made a resounding comeback to win.

Running back Mark Walton had 52 rushing yards and 17 carries in the 2016 Russell Athletic Bowl. He finished the 2016 season with 1,357 total yards for the Hurricanes.

The Coaches

Manny Diaz introduced a tradition called the "**Turnover Chain**" during the 2017 season. Defensive players who force a turnover during a game get to wear a thick chain made of **gold.** It has a centerpiece encrusted with orange and green **sapphires**.

Manny Diaz was defensive coordinator under Miami head coach Richt from 2016 to 2018. When Mark Richt retired, Diaz returned to Miami to replace him.

The Miami Hurricanes have had many head coaches since the football team began. Some have stayed for a long time, while others have stayed for only a season or two. The Hurricanes' first coach was Howard "Cub" Buck. Many of Miami's coaches only led the team for a few years. Current coach Manny Diaz is the team's 25th head coach.

ANDY GUSTAFSON Andy Gustafson was the head coach of the Miami Hurricanes from 1948 to 1963. These years were called the "Glory Years" of Hurricanes football. During Gustafson's time as coach, the team played in four bowl games. Nine of his players earned first team All-America status. Gustafson has the longest tenure and the most wins of any Hurricanes coach ever.

DENNIS ERICKSON Dennis Erickson was the 18th coach of the Hurricanes. He served as coach from 1989 to 1994. Erickson won two National Championships in 1989 and 1991; three Big East championships in 1991, 1992, and 1994; and was named Big East coach of the year in 1991, 1992, and 1994. In 2005, Erickson was **inducted** into the UM Sports **Hall of Fame** as the only head coach with two national titles.

MARK RICHT On December 4, 2015, Mark Richt was named the head coach of the Miami Hurricanes. During his first season with the team, the Hurricanes won nine games and lost only four. Richt dramatically improved the team's defense. In 2016, Miami was ranked 26th in the nation. Just the year before, they had been ranked 69th. Richt was a Hurricane himself in college, and coached the University of Georgia for 15 years before returning to Miami. Richt retired from coaching in 2018.

The Mascot

Sebastian leads the team onto the field at the start of games. He also pumps up the crowd from the sidelines during games. His signature move is the "C-A-N-E-S" cheer, where he forms the letters with his body while the fans chant in unison.

The Miami Hurricanes' mascot is not a hurricane. Instead, it is an ibis named Sebastian. An ibis is a bird with a long, thin beak and long legs. According to folklore, other birds look to the ibis as storms approach. The ibis is the last to disappear before the storm and the first to reappear after it ends. The ibis is seen as a symbol of leadership and bravery.

The ibis became the Hurricanes' team mascot in 1926. The first Sebastian costume debuted in 1958 during a football game. It was made and worn by a student named John Stormont. Stormont made the costume himself for $30 and portrayed Sebastian for the rest of the 1958 season. The mascot was named after Stormont's dormitory, San Sebastian Hall. Today's Sebastian costume is based on the one Stormont made.

With the exception of the years between 1984 and 1992, when he was portrayed by a UM staff member, Sebastian the Ibis has been played by a student. Sebastian has his own Instagram, Facebook, and Twitter accounts, and is even featured in the University of Miami's online campus directory.

Legends of the Past

For many players, their time with the Hurricanes is the start of a promising football career. These are some of the best-known football players to play for the University of Miami.

Jim Otto

Jim Otto joined the Miami Hurricanes in 1957. He quickly became a star of the team, playing both center and middle linebacker. During his time at Miami, Otto set a school record for career tackles. After playing for the Miami Hurricanes for three years, Otto signed with the Oakland Raiders in 1960. He played 308 games over 15 seasons with the Raiders. He retired from pro football in 1974. In 1980, Otto became the first Hurricane to be inducted into the Pro Football Hall of Fame.

Position: Center
Seasons: 1957–1959 (Miami Hurricanes), 1960–1974 (Oakland Raiders)
Born: January 5, 1938, Wausau, Wisconsin

Bennie Blades

Bennie Blades began playing with the Miami Hurricanes in 1985. In 1987, he received the Jim Thorpe Award, naming him college football's best defensive back. That same year, Blades led the Hurricanes to the National Championship with a 12–0 record. At the end of his UM career, Blades was the all-time leader for interceptions and interception return yards. After he graduated from Miami, Blades was drafted by the NFL's Detroit Lions, and played with them for nine years. Blades played his final pro season in 1997 with the Seattle Seahawks.

Position: Safety
Seasons: 1985–1987 (Miami Hurricanes), 1988–1996 (Detroit Lions), 1997 (Seattle Seahawks)
Born: September 3, 1966, Fort Lauderdale, Florida

Adrian Colbert

Adrian Colbert spent his first three years of college at the University of Texas playing football for the Longhorns before transferring to Miami for his senior year. At Miami, Colbert played in seven games and missed six due to injuries. In October 2016, Colbert had a high of six tackles in a game against the Virginia Tech Hokies. Although he was not a first pick in the draft, Colbert has shown himself to be a powerful player and a great asset to the San Francisco 49ers, where he has played since 2017.

Position: Defensive Back
Seasons: 2013–2015 (Texas Longhorns),
2016 (Miami Hurricanes),
2017–Present (San Francisco 49ers)
Born: October 6, 1993, Mineral Wells, Texas

Denzel Perryman

Denzel Perryman played in every game during the 2011 season, his freshman year with the Hurricanes. That season, he recorded a career high of 14 tackles in one game. Perryman's impressive beginning foreshadowed the rest of his career. In 2013, he led the Hurricanes with 108 total tackles. He became renowned for stopping players in their tracks. Perryman was drafted by the NFL's San Diego Chargers in 2015, which later became the Los Angeles Chargers. In 2016, he led the team with 80 tackles and continues to be a valuable part of the Chargers' defense.

Position: Linebacker
Seasons: 2011–2014 (Miami Hurricanes),
2015–Present (Los Angeles Chargers)
Born: December 5, 1992, Miami, Florida

All-Time Records

35

Career Touchdowns

Edgerrin James scored 35 touchdowns for the Hurricanes, a record he tied in 1998. James also holds the UM record for the most single games completing 100 or more rushing yards, with 14.

77

Single-Game Points

On September 21, 2013, the Hurricanes scored 77 points in a game against Savannah State University, the most they have scored in any single game.

527

Single-Season Points

In 2002, the Hurricanes scored 527 points during the season, the most ever for Miami.

279

Single-Season Pass Completions

During the 1984 season, the Hurricanes made 279 pass completions, the most of any season for the team.

403

Most Points in a Career

Between 2014 and 2017, Michael Badgley scored a record 403 total points in his career with the Hurricanes.

Throughout the team's history, the Miami Hurricanes have had many memorable events that have become defining moments for the team and its fans.

1900 | 1920 | 1940 | 1960

1926
The Miami Hurricanes play their first game.

In 1933, the Canes play in their first bowl game, the Palm Festival.

1937
The Hurricanes win their first Southern Intercollegiate Athletic Association Championship.

1948
Andy Gustafson becomes the head coach.

1966
The Hurricanes sign their first African American player, Ray Bellamy.

The Future

Even though the team has not won a national title since 2001, the Miami Hurricanes continue to sign talented players. The Hurricanes finished the 2017 season 13th in the nation and have won the right to play in a postseason bowl game for six-straight seasons since 2013. Manny Diaz brings two decades of special teams coaching experience to Miami. The team's defense has been one of the best in the nation under Diaz, and his devotion to the Hurricanes will lead the team to a great future.

1983
UM wins the National Championship.

2003
UM loses the Fiesta Bowl to Ohio State and does not continue to the National Championship game.

1980 — 2000 — 2020

On Jan 1, 1988, Miami wins its second National Championship in five years.

2017
Nine Hurricanes are selected in the NFL draft, the most since 2006.

1992
Hurricane Andrew ravages South Florida, and the Hurricanes have to move 200 miles (320 km) north to Vero Beach, Florida, for their preseason drills.

2018
Mark Richt retires and Manny Diaz takes over as head coach.

Write a Biography

Life Story

A person's life story can be the subject of a book. This kind of book is called a biography. Biographies often describe the lives of people who have achieved great success. These people may be alive today, or they may have lived many years ago. Reading a biography can help you learn more about a great person.

Get the Facts

Use this book, and research in the library and on the internet, to find out more about your favorite player. Learn as much about him as you can. What position does he play? What are his statistics in important categories? Has he set any records? Also, be sure to write down key events in the person's life. What was his childhood like? What has he accomplished off the field? Is there anything else that makes this person special or unusual?

Use the Concept Web

A concept web is a useful research tool. Read the questions in the concept web on the following page. Answer the questions in your notebook. Your answers will help you write a biography.

Concept Web

Write a Biography

Adulthood
- Where does this individual currently reside?
- Does he have a family?

Your Opinion
- What did you learn from the books you read in your research?
- Would you suggest these books to others?
- Was anything missing from these books?

Childhood
- Where and when was this person born?
- Describe his parents, siblings, and friends.
- Did this person grow up in unusual circumstances?

Accomplishments off the Field
- What is this person's life's work?
- Has he received awards or recognition for accomplishments?
- How have this person's accomplishments served others?

Help and Obstacles
- Did this individual have a positive attitude?
- Did he receive help from others?
- Did this person have a mentor?
- Did this person face any hardships?
- If so, how were the hardships overcome?

Accomplishments on the Field
- What records does this person hold?
- What key games and plays have defined his career?
- What are his stats in categories important to his position?

Work and Preparation
- What was this person's education?
- What was his work experience?
- How does this person work?
- What is the process he uses?

Trivia Time

Take this quiz to test your knowledge of the Miami Hurricanes. The answers are printed upside down under each question.

1 What is the Hurricanes' mascot? What is the mascot's name?

A. An ibis, Sebastian

2 What is the name of the Hurricanes' home stadium?

A. Hard Rock Stadium

3 What year did the Hurricanes play their first game?

A. 1926

4 How many fans attended the Hurricanes' first game?

A. 304

5 When did the Hurricanes win their first National Championship?

A. 1983

6 Who is the Hurricanes' current head coach?

A. Manny Diaz

7 What are the University of Miami's school colors?

A. Green, orange, and white

8 Which coach stayed with the Hurricanes the longest?

A. Andy Gustafson

9 What was the name of the first bowl game the Hurricanes played?

A. The Palm Festival

10 What stopped construction on the Hurricanes' first stadium?

A. A hurricane

Key Words

draft: an annual event where the NFL chooses college football players to be new team members

Hall of Fame: a group of persons judged to be outstanding in a particular sport

integrated: when people of different races are allowed to be together in a certain place or group

inducted: added as an official member of a group

legends: extremely well-known people or events

logo: a symbol that stands for a team or organization

postseason: a sporting event that takes place after the end of the regular season

renovation: construction that works to improve or expand an older building

rivals: groups or individuals who compete toward the same objective or goal

segregated: when people of different races are not allowed to be together in a certain place or group

Super Bowl: the NFL's annual championship game between the winning team from the National Football Conference and the winning team from the American Football Conference

Index

Log on to www.av2books.com

AV² by Weigl brings you media enhanced books that support active learning. Go to www.av2books.com, and enter the special code found on page 2 of this book. You will gain access to enriched and enhanced content that supplements and complements this book. Content includes video, audio, weblinks, quizzes, a slideshow, and activities.

AV² Online Navigation

Audio
Listen to sections o
the book read alou

Book Pages
AV² pages directly correspond to pages in the book.

Video
Watch informative video clips.

Embedded Weblinks
Gain additional information for research.

Key Words
Study vocabulary, and complete a matching word activity.

Try This!
Complete activities and hands-on experiments.

Quizzes
Test your knowledge.

Slideshow
View images and captions, and prepare a presentation.

AV² was built to bridge the gap between print and digital. We encourage you to tell us what you like and what you want to see in the future.

Sign up to be an AV² Ambassador at www.av2books.com/ambassador.

Due to the dynamic nature of the internet, some of the URLs and activities provided as part of AV² by Weigl may have changed or ceased to exist. AV² by Weigl accepts no responsibility for any such changes. All media enhanced books are regularly monitored to update addresses and sites in a timely manner. Contact AV² by Weigl at 1-866-649-3445 or av2books@weigl.com with any questions, comments, or feedback.